This publication was supported
by a grant from the Greenwall Fund
of the Academy of American Poets

surfaces

surfaces

John Tipton

Flood Editions
Chicago 2004

for permission, required to reprint or broadcast more than
several lines, write to: Flood Editions, Post Office Box 3865,
Chicago, Illinois 60654-0865   www.floodeditions.com

ISBN 0-9746902-0-1

book design by Richard Eckersley   images by Jeff Marlin
typeset in Adobe Myriad MM   printed on acid-free paper
printed in the United States of America by Thomson-Shore

FIRST EDITION

for Stephanie,
of course

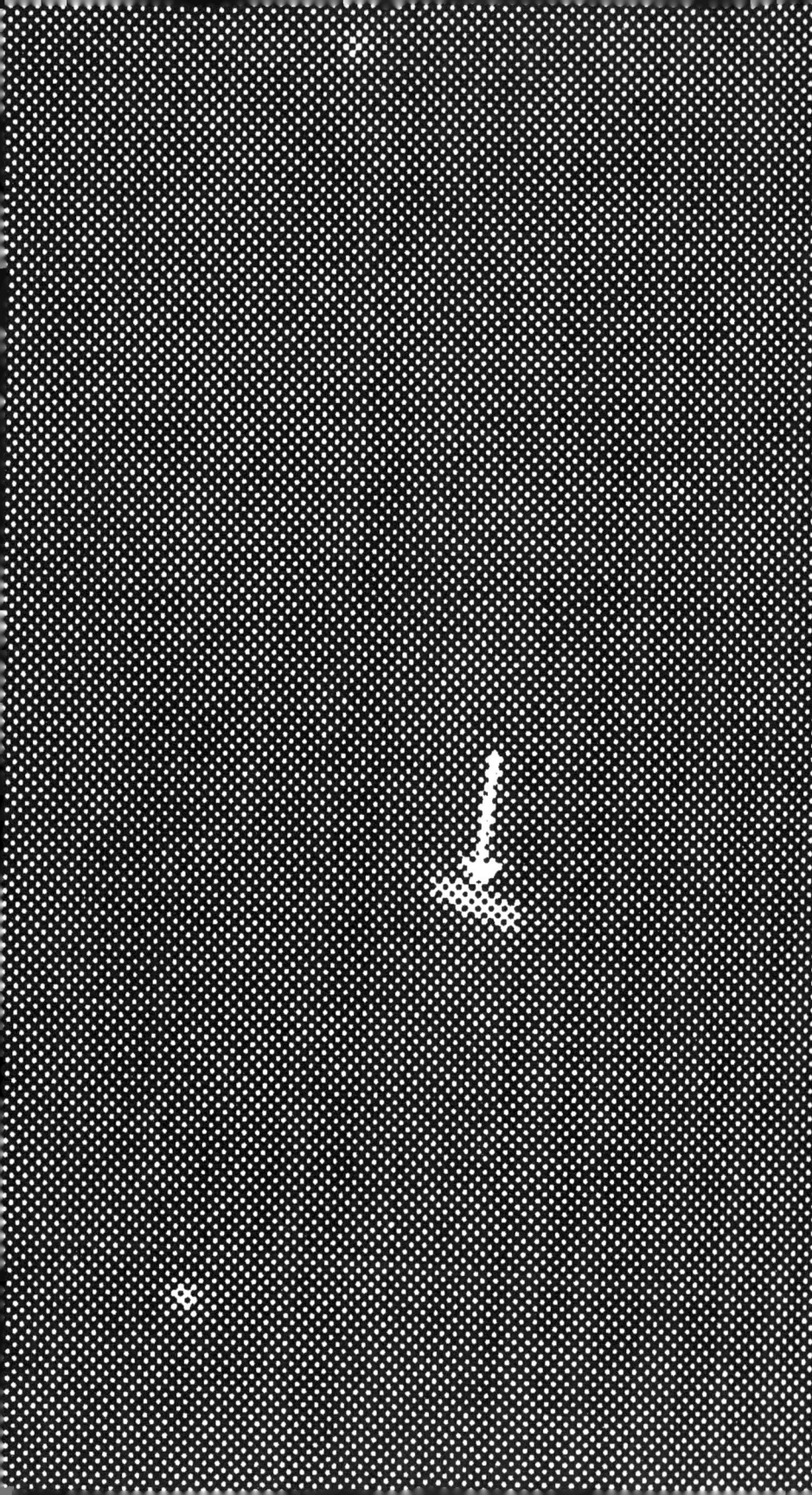

contents

flat

for Jeff Marlin

here the horizon is the geography here
Oklahoma moves him in ways he forgets

A. Square imagines textures & reads
Quine with the fervor of the flat

all that there is is the plane
so he now knows after philosophy's end

here the geography is the horizon here
Oklahoma moves him in ways he regrets

Square lands in Tulsa at 2:37 PM
to present a short talk on time

three hours & 14 minutes after arrival
he's driving a Pontiac to Oklahoma City

as Square drives west he ruminates that
stacking things is a form of prayer

listens to the ballgame for 50 miles
someone's got a curveball they call epilepsy

in his head he's charted every pitch
puts the entire game into a list

*

no longer driving he's on a raft
of sycamore floating down the sparkling highway

mottled by the shadows of the clouds
the plain absorbs the light like ink

dips his hand, troubles the illegible lines
of a newspaper bleeding onto the pavement

the page blotted & stained with rain
reveals the riddle of the true reader

A. Square takes an approach called liminalism
treating each English word as a threshold

chalks the flat tree of a sentence
onto a colorless blackboard in his brain

the surface is bright—no question but
who will it bridge the gap without?

afraid to imagine a town where tornadoes
this he's paralyzed at the thought of

the truth is somewhere further to the west
Los Angeles maybe—he's never been there

*

on the radio just past Exit 12
Sonny Rollins in goatee & dark glasses

squawking his way through *Night in Tunisia*
picking out the notes he finds salient

the melody frays into jammed tattered phrases
like a letter from an ancient author

one from Tully to his brother Quintus
full of opaque idioms & inside jokes

how that letter would have been read
on a gray March day in Munich

read perhaps by Ockham   how he'd smile
what could he possibly find amusing here?

then back at the wheel in Oklahoma
ragged fireball sun consumed   Square sped west

the car flushed a pair of quail
who clapped & battered their way aloft

jet crickets wrinkled the weatherless August twilight
curtaining the unseen border of the night

syntax at Moab

that sky extends its bounds by nine
's not captured in the weather predicate

is it gypsum makes the desert shine?
this sun gives absence in discrete terms

it blocks the pathway of the said
wouldn't let [$_{IP}$ her [$_I$ Ø] [$_{VP}$ [$_V$ speak] each word]]

there discovers the thief of the infinitive
where dryness forms the grain of atmospheres

what did those words drift like ravens
as we repeat them seven years ago?

this question marks the place it departs
& begs movement of the spectacular clouds

it tried T. to hear transitive gestures
& the minimal not & bothers him

but everyone describes a picture of herself
imagines the slant rain a glance blurs

what jointed phrase we'll have, my dear
while our clauses crack in the afternoon

Utah severs to remember & drops apart
the tense that we use not saying

we cannot unlearn to think what portions
the choice of things bare & keen

patterns

1

speech in the desert leaves a film
it's trapped on the surface of patterns

take this path to the next fork
where it assigns case to the noun

we will make ecology in the branches
the line's last word should be true

here we invoke Nagasaki — how many died?
does a fractal simulation of the blast

the history of choices forms a tree
factual & horrible stem from one root

each branch bends from decision to decision
from verbless lines to conceptions of semantics

coarse bark grades in lieu of grain
touch wends through the texture of trees

the oarsman rowed through the locks drowned.
but who rowed him through the locks?

make proteins with the structure of sentences
write phrases in the shape of time

after the translation gave us extra syllables
she sang *Radix of Goodness* off key

2

that a question is a broken ring
hemmed in by ordinary language is false

music doesn't branch so much as turn
you hear the limitations of the recording

help me locate language in the genome
have you heard what's been going around?

set formed by everything five kilometers away
rings & other circular technologies remained undiscovered

sunday monday tuesday wednesday thursday friday saturday
the lengths we go to to describe

the poem returns to an earlier theme,
lifts off the water, circles, & disappears

the rings of Saturn: ☐ ☐ ☐
are we still talking about the world?

Christoph is lost in the sun's disk
looking for spots drifting across its face

he will study mechanical descriptions of reality
called 'philosophy' or 'the comfort of letters'

in Greek, time rubs, but in English
the calendar will come back as rain

3

sky points in the instance of rain
the grid does not unify it dismembers

Paul Celan drowned himself in the Seine
in an attempt to make expression precise

he talks about the direction of time
but he only mentions what happened before

whether she plays chess or writes poems
move toward the end of the utterance

an insect leads us to the corner
it maneuvers through a patch of light

where we start I don't know where
'wanders around for a while' says nothing

the four corners of the verb absorb
a grammar as a set of rules

he used x's to indicate his fingers
& said machine to designate a system

T. mused what this puzzle might imply
& said significant when he meant referent

you take in at a glance that
strings are blind but arrows have sight

4

speaking on the phone from Florida yesterday
my father lost his train of thought

he couldn't remember how to represent e
which is not a letter from friends

this letter tells us we have cancer
sender and receiver on the same line

she laughed at the violin's thin song
something about the linear order of sentences

she finds relief in the false lemma
which says threads are not about time

your question twists into some odd corners
having trouble teasing sense out of it?

we built a model of a string
from verbs mumbled on the B train

it held his chest together with wire
it kept a scent on his hands

let's assume this section operates on strings
each sequence has a pace & pronunciation

it's a story much like any other
bound to the surface of the line

5

lonesome Omaha John hopped a coal train
outside Passaic after a night in Paterson

& he would never arrive anywhere again
even the Ohio highway where he died

he knew this one pulled no boxcars
to nap in on the way west

luckless Omaha John stood between two cars
as the train stitched the rails below

the coal dust taste in his mouth
removed all memory of that day's lunch

through the deafening cicadas some call locusts
John discerned a house across bean fields

a house of rooms teeming with insects
devouring the squared doors & pegged rafters

a house where no one sits writing
& no trace of thought is left

where no one witnesses ants searching through
a room with light on three sides

ants whose jaws mesh on boneless linkages
ants whose patterns are not their own

without reference

sound of rain wrapt in paper
silence in aspects of the ants
facts of them on the page
of their condition in a fold
facts of the sound of rain
a sparrow clatters in the thorns

this sparrow's noise in the thorns
the sound of rain on paper
sheet of paper in the rain
page gives cover to foraging ants
flightless insects trapped in the folds
in the state of the page

Euclid put features on his page
point at the cusp of thorn
thus A. Square knows no folds
Linus writes proteins on brown paper
you can't see claws on ants
if each line bends in rain

what it is of it rains
read hand waves pass through page
& counts legs as can ants
sums along in think tally thorn
clouds sit fracture when stain papers
brown is taste it cloves fold

in the quiet of a fold
writing at the pace of rain
Turing's machine shuttles on its paper
shuttles & encrypts its tape page
thorn is nothing if not thorn
it is as if an ant

at their fungus gardening the ants
crimp leaves that they will fold
into damp chambers beneath the thorns
slick leaves shudder in the rain
ants hide in a stray page
a sparrow jabs at the paper

paper pages ant   fold thorns rain
ant paper folds   thorn rains page
page ant thorns   fold rains paper

film

scene i
Night… Jack makes a silent documentary about army ants.

scene ii
He shoots corners of houses — calls it *The Catalog of Ships*.

scene iii
Sarah is too moved to talk, too scared to talk to.

scene iv
Who do you think visited Manfred as we warned her?

scene v
Jack's eye blurs.

scene vi
There seem to be shadow in the white envelope.

scene vii
It's Jack who Manfred tried to be filmed.

scene viii
the letters she shreds before reading

scene ix
There are most people watching.

scene x
Jack breaks Sarah the window as a warning.

scene xi
"With him were forty black ships."

[Omnes ad unum interficiuntur] fills the room
trades immense for matrix, hoof for noun
its oblong remnants taste steely & distilled
its pale marks left after the forage
& made believe the bad heel blindly
drew up boundaries & were so arrayed
through the window the token *thirst* appears
at dusk on a page with *scar*
it is not the smell of cinnamon
not the sun striking a mineral-red wall
that they adventure for none but themselves
if deciding the book to be obscure
—the cost of the coast of Sicily—
Caesar ait: Milites ad unum omnes interficiuntur.

there speaks a sentence no one understands
the man uttered it was a neighbor
where he lives the sentence next door
could not help but damage the sample
it waking lapses wounds the eye blue
this eye picks friends out of photos
yet memory dyes the sentence cannot end
he's stuck gaping—searching for a word
the mirror shaving loses hold this man
could not abstract himself from it sight
mechanical gaps open his vision & frighten
it no longer makes sense the mirror
& disappears with all its good contents
abandoned for terms that should mean ordinary

taxicab logic

1

stoplights form the grid of the possible
& comprise the T or F sentences

we're somewhere on the decision tree
that represents the way home from anywhere

the tree is its own city plan
the city is a theater of streets

cabs have names like 'bachelor & bride'
'defense of the hive' & 'Tarski's convention'

2

the geometry of thought is not conscious
I practice forgetting all kinds of things

let's use props with the zero-degree notation
same clothes in summer as in winter

rhythm is distance is the way home
from where we started on the radio

to where we end up on backseats
in alleys waiting for him to finish

3

the latitude of the Straits of Magellan
the idea little more than a figure

construction of poems that are not empty
poems that are faces on the page

train analogy for motion in one dimension
let's make a train—who's the caboose?

see the effect of lines in space
there's an invisible error in the figures

4 (experiment)

each cab driver has a watch which
may or may not tell correct time

place clocks at each corner throughout town
all clocks start with the correct time

as cabs pass, drivers check their watches
and set them to the clock's time

at every stop, the driver exits &
resets a clock to her watch's time

how long before all are wrong?
when will they be right again?

5

metonymy, he says, is a syntactic gesture
involving the lovely modulation of the type

though she insists on evaluating every letter
their sounds change from word to word

if numerals really were what they represented
if letters were more than a grid

alphabets are only an approximation of reading
it's a process of writing called concatenation

6

relate your story in rule-based terms or
the score's last movement will falter unforgivably

kinship between q, x, & the checkerboard
taxi silenced by e & soft g

takes us without interruption from one location
as if in a dream, quite unaware

the how of getting here from there
the where of all along the way

7

radio plays Wayne Shorter—something from Etc.
something wrong with the engine is wrong

drive to the gardens with the sour
smell of bark in the evergreen beds

cabs dodge umbrellas that litter the street
umbrellas upside down collecting rain from everywhere

ice

implication
direction
vector
sled
world that glares
is only surface
sheet of sky
an oblate sphere
the gravity contraption
that traps him
dogs drag sled
in the snow
on line south
until south disappears
14 December, 1911
Roald Amundsen occupies
latitude 90° S
asserts the truth
of his location
& its extremity
facts are world
as land expands
to its foundations
frame made visible
polar regions shine
horizon reduced to
its immediate signs
landscape assembles itself
bright & heatless
as an end
impossible & necessary
$p \rightarrow q$
smooth as proof
runner
arrow
if

pictures of snow

pictures of snow
lapse at spots
to unhide ink

snow no darker
than the sky
grays a raven

bird calls banks
stirs fixed point
drifts into trees

will weigh slender
the raw chink
the rooted frame

the snow's joints
number the unique
ways to fall

or still branch
or dead leaves
or some rust

raven give us
what falls orthogonal
what aligns vision

photos of ravens
have a gloss
of their own

52 surfaces

for Dan Habu (somewhat)
& Rob Davis (mostly)

1

how often have we spoken of branches in winter?

2

the snow never will end

3

bast$_1$ gore$_2$ ilk$_3$ cask$_4$ orb$_5$ quilt$_6$ scored$_7$ ooze$_8$ spurt$_9$

4

spellings must be countable

5

if our verbs agree our pain is translatable

6

glass blankly when you must road

7

she calls it the silence of diagrams

8
this is the line about all lines that aren't about themselves

9
[spool] → [heel] → [squish]

10
no one need ever read it in the original

11
etymology is another story

12
it tries to explain language in surfaces

13
$\bar{Q}$ is what this is called

14
Jasper Johns told me in a dream to cut off his hands

15
this is the beginning

16
black against snow

17

it would diagonalize out of our conversation

18

how often we have spoken of branches in winter

19

they made arrangements for the end of marriage

20

she would hear him sobbing in the wake of the last scene

21

the previous statement is false

22

someone spoke each metaphor

23

he has a book of all possible utterances

24

bottle is a phonic section

25

if I say 'market' this becomes a political poem

26
oaks & oxen & crows

27
everything depends on the size of the sample

28
it snows

29
M. Bourbaki writes a poem with arbitrarily long lines

30
carves brittle leaves of wood

31
& puts his cats in a sentence

32
At most, fifty-one of these are about themselves, or they all are.

33
this line is called the violence of the market

34
the tulips have collapsed on the pavement

35

this is the initial technology

36

whenever it snows he loses new memories

37

when he forgets enough he's no longer angry

38

If #32 is false, what can this mean?

39

Mr. Church has a machine that will translate your book

40

this one is for hiccups

41

this one is for the quality of light

42

#13 refers to the Q-bar theory

43

why are you so hung up on truth?

44
the argument hangs on this point

45
the lexical accident speaks perfect squares

46
a day without weather

47
'The necessary syntax' is not a sentence.

48
she gave us a method for turning all phrases into diagrams

49
who will lance Job's boils?

50
the man of steel?

51
I call this problem Job's boils

52
& so it snows

the falsework gave way beneath the falsework
a bridgeless space opens time is flat
light streams   falls   a lightwell forms
where nothing opens in the orange bridge
is neither evidence nor is it stable
an orange bridge is riveted in blue
& you begin to fall   you fell
you span the weave of bodily perfection
my bridge makes distance grammar, theory bend
the crows' calls as clear as speech
lose the glowing rivet to the glint
of a river purling fourhundred feet dark
there the skaters will glide come December
& your descent is true   is true

Dear Markov,

I counted the words that you asked
set them in rows took their logarithms
but there spoils the proof the words
the method yields a remainder but one
(of which window did they fall out?)
message decays with time yet remain messages
if we can number them by hand
what did string on the finger forget?
but something sits just under the phonetics
perhaps a submarine beneath the polar cap
blind & voiceless it echoes the cold
noun trapped inside which will slowly suffocate
before its spellings collapse & it implodes
have we become those tragic sailors, Andrei?

—Shannon

Good Shannon,

I see the method has misled you
when I say *method* you hear *map*
it approximates English never really being so
think in terms of atomic models, Claude
while you scruple the surface it glares
sound & sense seduce with their friction
what broken phrase is not to hear?
you seem as if someone is reading
just like Whorf & his fictive Eskimo
the ad hoc nonsense names for snow
you counted the words but you failed
to go & speak with that Eskimo
bent over a hole in the ice
waiting for anything to rise & breathe

—Markov

composition in 90 words

thread winds clockwise
black to white
through the air

made of fiber
as dark as
blood in urine

chair binds thread
on rungs from
number to floor

where terse ends
fray yet attach
at each point

chair of each
point links to
floor by thread

set of points
in the bundle
of real numbers

the thread map
is onto &
one to one

at one remove
from now from
sever & here

threads are scars
in the gap
between two things

a boundary clue
into the skyless
into the empty

empty lot of the Red Steel tavern
distressed in halogen hush — cinder block building
Shadwell the seller the dope from Amsterdam
the dollar bill who marks who passes
who would the fact police arrested amaze
Shadwell so they wonder whether was killed
the mayor it seems to himself compromised
there was the body you couldn't find
papers carried it to a strip shop
on the West Side where radios play
if Breen left Shadwell the trunk unlocked
how carefully didn't the wire give facts
police worded the ransom tenderly for TV
's promise of photos hushed the crowd

barriers

who numbers of are imagined
who pictures of are on fire
who books of are unread

Dedekind occupies his room on the second floor
counts the lark prints on the bridge
Dedekind makes numbers in the region of words

what did you make pictures of
Dedekind wants that pictures of snow be on sale
what are pictures of on sale

who did you cross a bridge that built
what book altered you before you read
did you cross a bridge that who built

Dedekind tunnels a method
the bright cloud speeds south across the sky
through ladders of twelve

light leaks into the tunnel
gathers the shadowed
affinity between 5 & k

the section of the storm
that you met a man who talked about through the night
resembled the rest of winter

who did you read a book that wrote
the perfection of language
it cracked the palate at the thought of

unable to write
he forms words with the game pieces
patterned in wood

for whom is poetry
in ribbons
did you not read

Notes & Acknowledgments

without reference
The title comes from Donald Davidson's essay "Reality Without Reference."

"Dear Markov"
Andrei Markov, 1856–1922, Russian mathematician. Discovered sequences of random variables later known as the Markov chains. These in turn informed a mathematical tool known as the Hidden Markov Model.

"Good Shannon"
Claude Shannon, 1916–2001, American mathematician. Wrote *A Mathematical Theory of Communication* which employed Hidden Markov Models to analyze human language.

barriers
Richard Dedekind, 1831–1916, German mathematician. Developed a formal definition of the irrational numbers by making 'Dedekind Cuts' of the rational number line at irrational points. The poem takes its title from the Noam Chomsky monograph of the same name.

Some of these poems previously appeared in *Cello Entry*, *Chicago Review*, *LVNG*, *Nedge*, *New American Writing*, and on the Cultural Society web site. "52 surfaces" was published as a LVNG Supplementals broadside and "pictures of snow" appeared as a Cultural Society miniside. Many of these poems were previously collected in a chapbook, *clause automata* (Cello Entry, 2001).

I am in the debt of many people but there are five poets who deserve particular mention here: special thanks to Joel Felix, Devin Johnston, Rick Snyder, Michael O'Leary, and the *lector primus*, Peter O'Leary. Both the book and I were improved by their friendship.

About the Author

John Tipton had an itinerant childhood in Indiana, Florida, Oklahoma, Louisiana, and Illinois. After a three-year stint in the U.S. Army, he attended the University of Chicago on the GI Bill where he earned an AB in philosophy. He currently lives in Chicago and curates the Chicago Poetry Project, a series of readings at the Chicago Public Library.